Reptiles

BY MICHELLE LEVINE

amicus
high interest

Amicus High Interest is an imprint of Amicus
P.O. Box 1329, Mankato, MN 56002
www.amicuspublishing.us

Library of Congress Cataloging-in-Publication Data
Levine, Michelle, author.
 Reptiles / Michelle Levine.
    pages cm. — (Animal kingdom)
 Summary: "An introduction to what characteristics animals in
the reptile animal class have and how they fit into the animal
kingdom"—Provided by publisher.
 Audience: Grade K to 3.
 Includes bibliographical references and index.
 ISBN 978-1-60753-476-1 (library binding) —
 ISBN 978-1-60753-623-9 (ebook)
 1. Reptiles—Juvenile literature. I. Title.
 QL644.2.L48 015
 597.9—dc23
                                          2013031392

Editor: Wendy Dieker
Series Designer: Kathleen Petelinsek
Book Designer: Heather Dreisbach
Photo Researcher: Kurtis Kinneman

Photo Credits: Eduardo Grund/age fotostock/SuperStock,
cover; kungverylucky/Shutterstock, 5; Eric Isselee, 6;
Wayne Lynch/All Canada Photos/SuperStock, 9; Worraket/
Shutterstock, 10; Danita Delimont/Alamy, 13; Andi Erik/
Alamy, 14; Katrina Leigh, 17; Stock Connection/SuperStock,
18; blickwinkel/Alamy, 21; noppharat/Shutterstock, 22;
Animals Animals/SuperStock, 25; vikau, 26; Alena Brozova/
Shutterstock, 29

Printed in the United States of America at Corporate Graphics
in North Mankato, Minnesota.

10 9 8 7 6 5 4 3 2 1

Table of Contents

What Is a Reptile? 4

Eat or Be Eaten 11

Living on Land and in Water 16

Making Babies 20

Reptiles in the World 27

Glossary 30

Read More 31

Websites 31

Index 32

What Is a Reptile?

Chomp! A crocodile catches a fish. Hiss! A snake warns an enemy. Splash! A turtle slips into a pond. Zoom! A lizard runs from danger. These animals do not all look alike. And they do not all live in the same places. But they belong to the same animal **class**. They are all reptiles.

A crocodile is one of the largest reptiles. It hides so it can catch its next meal.

Take a close look at a snake's scales. Scales help protect reptiles.

Q How many kinds of reptiles are there?

What makes all of these animals reptiles? They all have a backbone. And most of them lay eggs. All reptiles are covered in **scales** too. The scales are tough and dry. They are made of the same thing as your fingernails. They protect a reptile's body.

 More than 9,500 kinds of reptiles live on Earth.

Reptiles are **cold-blooded**. Their bodies match the temperature around them. Reptiles **bask** to warm up. You might find a garter snake lying out in the sun. When they get too hot, they cool down in shady spots. Gila monsters dig tunnels underground to get out of the heat. Others slip into cool water or mud.

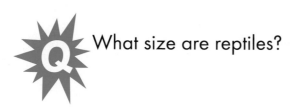

What size are reptiles?

A Gila monster comes out of its tunnel to warm up in the sun.

 The smallest could sit on the tip of your finger. One of the largest is the Komodo dragon. It can grow to 10 feet (3 m) long.

Many lizards eat insects.
This gecko caught a cricket.

 Are all reptiles carnivores?

Eat or Be Eaten

Gulp! A snake swallows a mouse. Most reptiles are **carnivores**. They hunt and eat other animals. Reptiles eat bugs, fish, and birds. They eat mammals and reptiles too. They also eat animal eggs. But most of them don't have good teeth for chewing. Others have no teeth at all. These reptiles swallow their food whole.

No. Some are **herbivores**. They eat plants. Most tortoises are herbivores. So are many turtles.

Reptiles must watch out for **predators**. Their color helps them stay safe. Many reptiles blend into their surroundings. Reptiles also run from danger. Lizards are very fast. But what if a predator catches a lizard's tail? The lizard can shed its tail to get free. A new tail will grow back.

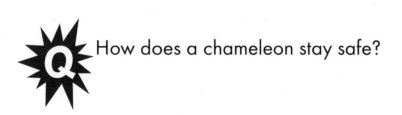 How does a chameleon stay safe?

This lizard runs fast to stay safe. It can even run on water!

 It changes color! Some kinds of chameleons change to match their surroundings.

Many reptiles hide from predators. They dig holes in dirt or sand. Or they sink underwater. Turtles and tortoises hide inside their hard shell.

Other reptiles fight. Snakes bite enemies with their teeth. Some snakes also make poison. It comes out of their sharp **fangs**. The poison harms or kills other animals.

A turtle hides in its shell.

Living on Land and in Water

Many reptiles live in warm or hot places.
Rain forests and deserts make good homes.
So do dry grasslands. Reptiles also live
in lakes, rivers, and the sea. But they can
live almost anywhere. Some live in cold
or wet places. Others live in mountains or
in trees.

Many reptiles make a
home in warm deserts.

Garter snakes come out from their den. They hibernate all winter.

Q How do reptiles breathe?

Why do reptiles like warm places? It's because they are cold-blooded. Their bodies don't work well in cold weather. They become slow and sleepy.

Some reptiles **hibernate** in winter. They crawl under a log or rock. Or they go into holes underground. Many turtles sink underwater. They come out again in spring.

They breathe air like you do. But some turtles can also breathe underwater.

Making Babies

Many reptiles **mate** in spring. Others mate in summer or fall. The males and females send messages to each other. They give off a special scent. They do a kind of dance. Or they show off colorful parts of their bodies. These messages say, "Let's get together!"

Almost all reptiles lay eggs. Cobras will hatch from this nest of eggs.

Q How many eggs do reptiles lay?

Female reptiles lay eggs after mating. Some lay eggs with hard shells. Others lay eggs with soft shells. The shells are like thick skin. Reptile eggs are a tasty treat for hungry predators. So mothers hide their eggs. They lay them in holes. Or they hide them in nests on the ground.

 Some reptiles lay only one or two eggs. Sea turtles can lay more than 100.

Soon babies hatch out of their eggs. Many reptile eggs take one to three months to hatch. But an iguana's eggs may take up to a year. Most reptile mothers do not stay with their eggs. The babies must care for themselves. They find their own food. And they stay away from danger.

Baby iguanas hatch and begin life on their own.

Reptiles eat pests that might harm a farmer's crops.

Q How long do reptiles live?

Reptiles in the World

Reptiles around the world help humans in many ways. They eat bugs and mice that harm crops. Rattlesnake poisons can be turned into medicines. Reptiles are also a source of food for some people. And they are food for other animals too.

 It depends on the reptile. Some live only two or three years. The giant tortoise can live more than 150 years.

Some reptiles are in danger. People have hunted too many of them. The wild places where reptiles live have also been harmed. And that harms the animals. Some kinds of reptiles have even gone **extinct**. People are working to protect reptiles and their homes. That way, these animals will be around for a long time.

Trash on the ground harms reptile homes.

Glossary

bask To lie in the sun to soak up heat.

carnivore A meat-eating animal.

class A group of animals that share similar characteristics.

cold-blooded An animal whose body temperature matches the air around it.

extinct Died out.

fangs The long pointy teeth of a poisonous snake.

herbivore A plant-eating animal.

hibernate To sleep during winter.

mate To come together to make babies.

predator An animal that hunts other animals for food.

scales Overlapping hard plates that cover a reptile's body.

Read More

Cleary, Brian. *Tortoise, Tree Snake, Gator, and Sea Snake: What Is a Reptile?* Minneapolis: Millbrook Press, 2013.

de la Bedoyere, Camilla. *Fearsome Reptiles.* Mankato, Minn: QEB Publishing, 2012.

Schuetz, Kari. *Reptiles.* Minneapolis: Bellwether Media, 2013.

Websites

Reptile Printouts: Enchanted Learning
http://www.enchantedlearning.com/subjects/reptiles/printouts.shtml

San Diego Zoo Kids: Reptiles
http://kids.sandiegozoo.org/animals/reptiles

Video: Reptiles: National Geographic Kids
http://video.nationalgeographic.com/video/kids/animals-pets-kids/reptiles-kids

Every effort has been made to ensure that these websites are appropriate for children. However, because of the nature of the Internet, it is impossible to guarantee that these sites will remain active indefinitely or that their contents will not be altered.

Index

babies 24

backbone 7

basking 8

breathing 18, 19

carnivores 10, 11

cold-blooded 8, 19

color 12, 20

crocodile 4

eggs 7, 11, 22, 23, 24

extinction 28

habitats 16, 19

herbivores 11

hibernation 19

humans 27, 28

lizards 4, 12, 24

mating 20, 23

poison 15, 27

predators 12, 15, 23

scales 7

size 8, 9

snakes 4, 8, 11, 15

tails 12

teeth 11, 15

tortoises 15

turtles 4, 15, 19

About the Author

Michelle Levine has written and edited many nonfiction books for children. She loves learning about new things—like reptiles—and sharing what she's learned with her readers. She lives in St. Paul, Minnesota.

4-15-15